# THE SAYINGS OF
# MAHATMA GANDHI

GRAHAM BRASH, SINGAPORE

*Generations to come, it may be,*
*will scarce believe that such a*
*one as this in flesh and*
*blood walked upon this earth*

**ALBERT EINSTEIN *on* GANDHI**

©Selection and arrangement of quotations,
Peter H. Burgess, 1984
Illustrations by Heng Kim Song

First published in 1984 by Graham Brash (Pte) Ltd


First reprinted 1990

Second reprinted 2000

ISBN 9812180788

Printed in Singapore

# Contents

# The Mahatma on Himself and his wife, Kasturibai

I WAS born at Porbandar, otherwise known as Sudamapuri, on the 2nd of October, 1869. I passed my childhood at Porbandar. I recollect having been put to school. It was with some difficulty that I got through the multiplication tables. The fact that I recollect nothing more of those days than having learnt, in company with other boys, to call our teachers all kinds of names, would strongly suggest that my intellect must have been sluggish and my memory raw.

I USED to be very shy and avoided all company. My books and my lessons were my sole companions. To be at school at the stroke of the hour and to run home as soon as the school closed - that was my daily habit. I literally ran back, because I could not bear to talk to anybody. I was even afraid lest anyone should poke fun at me.

MOVEOVER, I was a coward. I did not dare to stir out of doors at night. Darkness was a terror to me. It was almost impossible for me to sleep in the dark, as I would imagine ghosts coming from one direction, thieves from another and serpents from a third. I could not therefore bear to sleep without a light in the room.

How could I disclose my fears to my wife, no child, but already at the threshold of youth, sleeping by my side? I knew that she had more courage than I, and I felt ashamed of myself. She knew no fears of serpents and ghosts. She could go out anywhere in the dark.

I WANTED to *make* my wife an ideal wife. My ambition was to *make* her live a pure life, learn what I learnt, and identify her life and thought with mine.

I do not know whether Kasturibai had any such ambitions. She was illiterate. By nature she was simple, independent, persevering, and, with me at least, reticent. She was not impatient of her ignorance and I do not recollect my studies having spurred her to go in for a similar adventure. I fancy, therefore, that my ambition was all one-sided. My passion was entirely centred on one woman, and I wanted it to be reciprocated. But even if there was no reciprocity, it could not be all unrelieved misery because there was active love on one side at least.

I MUST say I was passionately fond of her. Even at school I used to think of her, and the thought of nightfall and our subsequent meeting was ever haunting me. Separation was unbearable. I used to keep her awake till late at night with my idle talk. If with this devouring passion there had not been with me a burning attachment to duty, I should either have fallen a prey to disease and premature death, or have sunk into a burdensome existence ... I have already said that Kasturibai was illiterate. I was very anxious to teach her, but lustful love left me no time. For one thing the teaching had to be done against her will, and that too at night ... I must therefore confess that most of my efforts to instruct Kasturibai in our youth were unsuccessful. And when I awoke from the sleep of lust, I had already launched forth into public life, which did not leave me much spare time.

*(Gandhi and Kasturibai were married when they were both thirteen.)*

I AM sure that had my love for her been absolutely untainted with lust, she would be a learned lady today; for I could then have conquered her dislike for studies. I know that nothing is impossible for pure love.

... I SAID, raising my voice: 'I will not stand this nonsense in my house!'

She shouted back: 'Keep your house to yourself and let me go!' I forgot myself ... I caught her by the hand, dragged the helpless woman to the gate ... and proceeded to open it with the intention of pushing her out. The tears were running down her cheeks ... and she cried:

'Have you no sense of shame? ... Where am I to go? ... Being your wife, you think I must put up with your cuffs and kicks? For Heaven's sake behave yourself and shut the gate ...'

I ... was really ashamed and shut the gate. If my wife could not leave me, neither could I leave her.

I LEARNT the lesson of nonviolence from my wife, when I tried to bend her to my will. Her determined resistance to my will, on the one hand, and the quiet submission to the suffering my stupidity involved, on the other, ultimately made me ashamed of myself and cured me of my stupidity ... in the end, she became my teacher in nonviolence.

THROUGHOUT my life I have gained more from my critic friends than from my admirers, especially when the criticism was made in courteous and friendly language.

My hesitancy in speech, which was once an annoyance, is now a pleasure. Its greatest benefit has been that it has taught me the economy of words. I have naturally formed the habit of restraining my thoughts. And I can now give myself the certificate that a thoughtless word hardly ever escapes my tongue or pen. I do not recollect having had to regret anything in my speech or writing.

AT the time of writing I never think of what I have said before. My aim is not to be consistent with my previous statements on a given question, but to be consistent with the truth as it may present itself to me at a given moment. The result has been that I have grown from truth to truth; I have saved my memory an undue strain; and what is more, whenever I have been obliged to compare my writing even of fifty years ago with my latest, I have discovered no inconsistency between the two.

EVERY night whilst my hands were busy massaging my father's legs, my mind was hovering about the bedroom — and that too at a time when religion, medical science and commonsense alike forbade sexual intercourse. (That night) I was glad to be relieved from my duty and went straight to the bedroom ... My wife, poor thing, was asleep ... I woke her up.
*(Minutes later there was a knock on the door and a servant told young Gandhi that his father was dead.)* I felt deeply ashamed

and miserable. I ran to my father's room. I saw that, if animal passion had not blinded me, I should have been spared the torture of separation from my father during his last moments. He would have died in my arms.

The shame of my carnal desire, even at the critical hour of my father's death, is a blot I have never been able to efface or forget. My devotion to my parents was weighed and found unpardonably wanting because my mind was at the same moment in the grip of lust, and I had to pass through many ordeals before I could overcome it.

*(Both Gandhi and Kasturibai were 16 years old when Gandhi's father died in 1885.)*

I HAVE nothing new to teach the world. Truth and non-violence are as old as the hills. All I have done is to try experiments in both on as vast a scale as I could. In doing so, I have sometimes erred and learnt by my errors. Life and its problems have thus become to me so many experiments in the practice of truth and nonviolence ...

Well, all my philosophy, if it may be called by that pretentious name, is contained in what I have said. But you will not call it 'Gandhism'; there is no 'ism' about it. The scriptures have been quoted against my position, but I have held faster than ever to the position that truth may not be sacrificed for anything whatsoever. Those who believe in the simple truths I have laid down can propagate them only by living them.

SUCH power as I possess for working in the political field derived from my experiments in the spiritual field.

I BELIEVE in trusting. Trust begets trust. Suspicion is foul and only stinks. He who trusts has never yet lost in the world. A suspicious man is lost to himself and the world. Let those who have made of nonviolence a creed beware of suspecting opponents. Suspicion is the brood of violence. Nonviolence cannot but trust. I must, at any rate, refuse to believe anything against anybody ... unless I have absolute proof.

I AM a lover of my own liberty and so I would do nothing to restrict yours.

My nationalism is intense internationalism. I am sick of the strife between nations or religions.

I AM perhaps the happiest man on earth today. I have during these two months experienced boundless love. And now I find myself arrested although I bear no ill will to anybody and although I am the one man who can today preserve the peace in India as no other man can. My imprisonment therefore will show the wrongdoer in his nakedness. And he can do me no harm for my spirit remains calm and unruffled.

THE heart's earnest and pure desire is always fulfilled. In my own experience I have often seen this rule verified. Service of the poor has been my heart's desire, and it has always thrown me amongst the poor and enabled me to identify with them.

I HAD been wedded to a monogamous ideal ever since my marriage, faithfulness to my wife being part of my love of truth.

But it was in South Africa that I began to realize the importance of observing *brahmacharya* even with respect to my wife.

DID my faithfulness consist in making my wife the instrument of my lust? So long as I was the slave of lust, my faithfulness was worth nothing. To be fair to my wife, I must say that she was never the temptress. It was therefore the easiest thing for me to take the vow of *brahmacharya*, if only I willed it. It was my weak will or lustful attachment that was the obstacle.

IT became my conviction that procreation and the consequent care of children were inconsistent with public service.

SEEING, therefore, that I did not desire more children, I began to strive after self-control. There was endless difficulty in the task. We began to sleep in separate beds. I decided to retire to bed only after the day's work had left me completely exhausted. All these efforts did not seem to bear much fruit ....

AFTER full discussion and mature deliberation, I took the vow in 1906. I had not shared my thoughts with my wife until then, but only consulted her at the time of taking the vow. She had no objection. But I had great difficulty in making the final resolve. I had not the necessary strength. How was I to control my passions? The elimination of carnal relationship with one's wife seemed then a strange thing. But I launched forth with faith in the sustaining power of God ... As I look back upon the twenty years of the vow, I am filled with pleasure and wonderment ... Before the vow I had been open to being overcome by temptation at any moment. Now the vow was a sure shield against temptation. The great potentiality of *brahmacharya* became more and more patent to me.

MY darkest hour was when I was in Bombay a few months ago. It was the hour of my temptation. While I was asleep I suddenly felt as though I wanted to see a woman. Well, a man who had tried to rise superior to the instinct for nearly forty years was bound to be intensely pained when he had this frightful experience. I ultimately conquered the feeling, but I was face to face with the blackest moment of my life and if I had succumbed to it, it would have been my absolute undoing.

I AM not a visionary. I claim to be a practical realist.

THOSE who have at all followed my humble career, even superficially, cannot fail to observe that not a single act of my life has been done to the injury of any individual or nation. My nationalism, as my religion, is not exclusive but inclusive, and must be so consistently with the welfare of all life.

I claim no infallibility. I am conscious of having made Himalayan blunders, but I am not conscious of having made them intentionally toward any person or nation, or any life, human or subhuman.

I DO sometimes become extremely angry with myself but I also pray to be delivered from that devil and God has given me power to suppress my anger.

I HAVE learned through bitter experience the one supreme lesson to conserve my anger, and as heat conserved is transformed into energy, even so an anger controlled can be transmuted into a power which can move the world.

I AM a dreamer. I am, indeed, a practical dreamer. My dreams are not airy things. I want to convert my dreams into realities, as far as possible.

IF I had no sense of humour, I would long ago have committed suicide.

I AM an irrepressible optimist. No scientist starts his experiments with a faint heart. I belong to the tribe of Columbus and Stevenson, who hoped against hope in the face of the heaviest odds. The days of miracles are not gone. They will abide so long as God abides.

I HOLD myself to be incapable of hating any being on earth. By a long course of prayerful discipline, I have ceased for over forty years to hate anybody. I know this is a big claim; I make it in all humility.

BUT I can and do hate evil wherever it exists. I hate the system of government that the British people have set up in India. I hate the ruthless exploitation of India even as I hate from the bottom of my heart the hideous system of untouchability for which millions of Hindus have made themselves responsible. But I do not hate the domineering Englishman as I refuse to hate the domineering Hindus. I seek to reform them in all the loving ways that are open to me. My noncooperation has its roots not in hatred, but in love.

I CONSIDER myself a Hindu, Christian, Moslem, Jew, Buddhist, and Confucian.

YOU must watch my life, how I live, eat, sit, talk, behave in general. The sum total of all these in me is my religion.

IT is an unbroken torture to me that I am still so far from Him, who as I fully know, governs every breath of my life, and whose offspring I am. I know that it is the evil passions within me that keep me so far from Him, and yet I cannot get away from them.

I COULD not be leading a religious life unless I identified myself with the whole of mankind, and that I could not do unless I took part in politics.

MEN say that I am a saint losing myself in politics. The fact is that I am a politician trying my hardest to be a saint.

I CLAIM to be no more than an average man with less than average ability. Nor can I claim any special merit for such nonviolence or continence as I have been able to reach with laborious research. I have not the shadow of a doubt that any man or woman can achieve what I have, if he or she would make the same effort and cultivate the same hope and faith.

I MUST try to live in society and yet remain untouched by its pitfalls.

... THOUGH by disclaiming sainthood I disappoint the critic's expectations, I would have him give up his regrets by answering him that the politician in me has never dominated a single decision of mine, and if I seem to take part in politics, it is only because politics encircle us today like the coil of a snake from which one cannot get out, no matter how much one tries ... Quite selfishly, as I wish to live in peace in the midst of a bellowing howling around me, I have been experimenting with myself and my friends by introducing religion into politics .

THE only tyrant I accept in this world is the 'still small voice' within me.

I BELIEVE that if one man gains spiritually, the whole world gains with him; if one man falls, the whole world falls to that extent. I do not help opponents without at the same time helping myself and my co-workers.

I DO not seek redemption from the consequences of my sin. I seek to be redeemed from sin itself, or rather from the very thought of sin. Until I have attained that end, I shall be content to be restless.

I WOULD prefer total destruction of myself and my all to purchasing safety at the cost of my manhood.

HOW can I, who knows the body to be perishable and the soul to be imperishable, mourn over the separation of body from soul?

HAVE I that nonviolence of the brave within me? My death alone will show that. If someone killed me and I died with prayer for the assassin on my lips, and God's remembrance and consciousness of His living presence in the sanctuary of my heart, then alone would I be said to have had the nonviolence of the brave.

**HE Ram!** **(O God!)** *(Gandhi's last words, spoken at his assassination on January 30th, 1948.)*

# On Nonviolence and the Struggle for Freedom

MY ambition is no less than to convert the British people through nonviolence, and thus make them see the wrong they have done to India. I do not seek to harm your people (*i.e. the British*). I want to serve them even as I want to serve my own.

THE British want to put the struggle on the plane of machine guns where they have weapons and we do not. Our only assurance of beating them is putting the struggle on a plane where we have weapons and they have not.

I CAN retain neither respect nor affection for a government which has been moving from wrong to wrong in order to defend its immorality.

SUBMISSION, therefore, to a state wholly or largely unjust is an immoral barter for liberty.

I DO not believe in short-violent-cuts to success ... However much I may sympathize with and admire worthy motives, I am an uncompromising opponent of violent methods, even to serve the noblest causes ... Experience convinces me that permanent good can never be the outcome of untruth and violence.

I OBJECT to violence because when it appears to do good, the good is only temporary; the evil it does is permanent.

WE have to make truth and nonviolence not matters for mere individual practice but for practice by groups and communities and nations. That, at any rate, is my dream. I shall live and die in trying to realize it. My faith helps me to discover new truths every day.

NONVIOLENCE is the first article of my faith. It is also the last article of my creed.

IF blood be shed, let it be our blood. Cultivate the quiet courage of dying without killing. For man lives only by his readiness to die, if need be, at the hands of his brother, never by killing him.

THERE are eternal principles which admit of no compromise; and one must be prepared to lay down one's life in the practice of them.

THE world is sick to death of blood-spilling. It is seeking a way out of its miseries. I flatter myself that India's new unique method, nonviolence, may show the world the way out from all its violent turmoil.

A NONVIOLENT revolution is not a programme of seizure of power. It is a programme of transformation of relationships, ending in a peaceful transfer of power.

LIBERTY and democracy become unholy when their hands are dyed red with innocent blood.

HE who perishes sword in hand is no doubt brave; but he who faces death without raising his little finger is braver.

IF it is brave, as it is, to die as a man fighting against odds, it is braver still to refuse to fight and yet refuse to yield to the usurper.

... NONVIOLENCE is not a cloistered virtue to be practised by the individual for his peace and final salvation, but it is a rule of conduct for society ... To practise nonviolence in mundane matters is to know its true value. It is to bring heaven upon earth ... I hold it therefore to be wrong to limit the use of nonviolence to hermits for acquiring merit for a favoured position in the world. All virtue ceases to have use if it serves no purpose in every walk of life.

STRENGTH does not come from physical capacity. It comes from an indomitable will.

STRENGTH of numbers is the delight of the timid. The valiant of spirit glory in fighting alone. Be you one or many, this valour is the only true valour, all else is false. And the valour of the spirit cannot be achieved without Sacrifice, Determination, Faith, and Humility.

LET us all be brave enough to die the death of a martyr, but let no one lust for martyrdom.

I HAVE come to see, what I did not see so clearly before, that there is nonviolence in violence. This is the big change which has come about. I had not fully realized the duty of restraining a drunkard from doing evil, or killing a dog in agony or one infected with rabies. In all these instances, violence is in fact nonviolence.

NONVIOLENCE and truth are inseparable and presuppose one another. There is no god higher than truth.

MENTAL violence has no potency and injures only the person whose thoughts are violent. It is otherwise with mental nonviolence. It has a potency which the world does not yet know.

FREEDOM'S battles are not fought without paying heavy prices. Just as a man would not cherish the thought of living in a body other than his own, so nations do not like to live under other nations, however noble and great the latter may be.

IT is any day better to stand erect with a broken and bandaged head than to crawl on one's belly, in order to be able to save one's head.

HE is the true soldier who knows how to die and stand his ground in the midst of a hail of bullets. A soldier never worries as to what shall happen to his work after him but thinks only of the immediate duty in front of him.

HEROES are made in the hour of defeat. Success is, therefore, well described as a series of glorious defeats.

MEANS are not to be distinguished from ends. If violent means are used, there will be a bad result.

GLORY lies in the attempt to reach one's goal and not in reaching it.

THE simplest things have the knack sometimes of appearing to us the hardest. If our hearts were opened, we should have no difficulty.

Nonviolence is a matter of the heart. It does not come to us through any intellectual feat. Everyone has faith in God, though everyone does not know it. For, everyone has faith in himself and that multiplied to the *nth* degree is God.

THE moment the slave resolves that he will no longer be a slave, his fetters fall. He frees himself and shows the way to others. Freedom and slavery are mental states.

POLICIES may and do change. Nonviolence is an unchangeable creed. It has to be pursued in the face of violence raging around you.

IN this age of wonders, no one will say that a thing or an idea is worthless because it is new. To say it is impossible because it is difficult is again not in consonance with the spirit of the age. Things undreamt of are daily being seen, the impossible is ever becoming possible. We are constantly being astonished these days at the amazing discoveries in the field of violence. But I maintain that far more undreamt of and seemingly impossible discoveries will be made in the field of nonviolence.

FOR a nonviolent person, the whole world is one family. He will thus fear none, nor will others fear him.

IT is not nonviolence if we merely love those that love us. It is nonviolence only when we love those that hate us. I know how difficult it is to follow this grand law of love. But are not all great and good things difficult to do? Love of the hater is the most difficult of all. But by the grace of God even this most difficult thing becomes easy to accomplish if we want to do it.

TO lose patience is to lose the battle.

NONVIOLENCE with a nonviolent man is no merit. In fact it becomes difficult to say if it is nonviolence at all. But when it is pitted against violence, then one realizes the difference between the two. This we cannot do unless we are ever wakeful, ever vigilant, every striving.

HE who trembles or takes to his heels the moment he see two people fighting is not nonviolent, but a coward. A nonviolent person will lay down his life in preventing such quarrels.

NONVIOLENCE and cowardice go ill together. I can imagine a fully armed man to be at heart a coward. Possession of arms implies an element of fear, if not of cowardice. But true nonviolence is an impossibility without the possession of unadulterated fearlessness.

MY creed of nonviolence is an extremely active force. It has no room for cowardice or even weakness. There is hope for a violent man to be some day nonviolent, but there is none for a coward.

DISOBEDIENCE to be civil must be sincere, respectful, restrained, never defiant, must be based upon some well understood principle, must not be capricious and, above all, must have no ill will or hatred behind it.

AN unjust law is itself a species of violence. Arrest for its breach is more so.

CIVIL disobedience is the inherent right of the citizen. He dare not give it up without ceasing to be a man. Civil disobedience is never followed by anarchy. Every state puts down criminal disobedience by force. It perishes, if it does not. But to put down civil disobedience is to attempt to imprison the conscience.

NONVIOLENCE is not a garment to be put on and off at will. Its seat is in the heart and it must be an inseparable part of our very being.

I BESEECH you to realize the supreme importance of discipline. Let it not be said that we are a people incapable of maintaining discipline. Indiscipline will mean disaster and will make us like one who is pining to see independent India perish in sorrow and grief. We are as determined as ever to rule ourselves. It is for us to make the effort. The result will always be in God's hands.

THE great obstacle is that we have not yet emerged from the mobocratic stage. But my consolation lies in the fact that nothing is so easy as to train mobs, for the simple reason that they have no mind, no premeditation. They act in a frenzy. They repent quickly.

PHYSICAL possession of arms is the last necessity of the brave.

WHAT difference does it make to the dead, the orphans and the homeless, whether the mad destruction is wrought under the name of totalitarianism or the holy name of liberty or democracy?

I BELIEVE that a nation that is capable of limitless sacrifice is capable of rising to limitless heights.

NONVIOLENCE is the law of our species as violence is the law of the brute. The spirit lies dormant in the brute and he knows no law but that of physical might. The dignity of man requires obedience to a higher law — the strength of the spirit.

NATIONS are born out of travail and suffering.

IF we develop the force of will, we shall find that we do not need the force of arms.

NONVIOLENCE in its dynamic condition means conscious suffering. It does not mean meek submission to the will of the evil-doer, but it means the pitting of one's whole soul against the will of the tyrant. Working under this law of our being, it is possible for a single individual to defy the whole might of an unjust empire to save his honour, his religion, his soul, and lay the foundation for that empire's fall or its regeneration.

THE way of peace is the way of truth. Truthfulness is even more important than peacefulness.

WHENEVER you are confronted with an opponent, conquer him with love.

NONVIOLENCE is like radium in its action. An infinitesimal quantity of it embedded in a malignant growth acts continuously, silently and ceaselessly till it has transformed the whole mass of the diseased tissue into a healthy one. Similarly, even a little of true nonviolence acts in a silent, subtle, unseen way and leavens the whole of society.

THE cause of liberty becomes a mockery if the price to be paid is the wholesale destruction of those who are to enjoy liberty.

SUFFERING is the law of human beings, war is the law of the jungle. But suffering is infinitely more powerful than the law of the jungle for converting the opponent and opening his ears, which are otherwise shut to the voice of reason.

WE must rest satisfied with a knowledge only of the means and if these are pure, we can fearlessly leave the end to take care of itself.

THE goal ever recedes from us. The greater the progress, the greater the recognition of our own unworthiness. Satisfaction lies in the effort, not in the attainment. Full effort is full victory.

IN our new freedom we may make mistakes. Freedom is not worth having if it does not connote freedom to err and even to sin. If God has given the humblest of His creatures the freedom to err, it passes my comprehension how human beings, be they ever so experienced and able, can delight in depriving other human beings of that precious right.

At His Trial in 1917

*(Remarks made by Gandhi at his trial in 1917 in which he was accused and found guilty by the British of inciting sedition. The conviction was later set aside.)*

I HAVE no desire whatsoever to conceal from this court the fact that to preach disaffection towards the existing system of Government has become almost a passion with me.

LITTLE do town dwellers know how the semi-starved masses of India are slowly sinking to lifelessness. Little do they know that their miserable comfort represents the brokerage they get for the work they do for the foreign exploiter, that the profits and the brokerage are sucked from the masses. Little do they realize that the Government established by law in British India is carried on for the exploitation of the masses. No sophistry, no jugglery of figures, can explain away the evidence that the skeletons in many villages present to the naked eye.

I BELIEVE that I have rendered a service to India and England by showing in noncooperation the way out of the unnatural state in which both are living. In my opinion, noncooperation with evil is as much a duty as cooperation with good. But in the past, noncooperation has been deliberately expressed in violence to the evildoer. I am endeavouring to show to my countrymen that violent noncooperation only multiplies evil, and that as evil can only be sustained by violence, withdrawal of support for evil requires complete abstention from violence.

NONVIOLENCE implies voluntary submission to the penalty for noncooperation with evil. I am here, therefore, to invite and submit cheerfully to the highest penalty that can be inflicted upon me for what in law is deliberate crime, and what appears to me to be the highest duty of the citizen. The only course open to you, the judge and the assessors, is either to resign your posts and thus disassociate yourselves from evil, if you feel that the law you are called upon to administer is an evil, and that in reality I am innocent, or to inflict on me the severest penalty, if you believe that the system and the law you are assisting to administer are good for the people of this country, and that my activity is, therefore, injurious to the common weal.

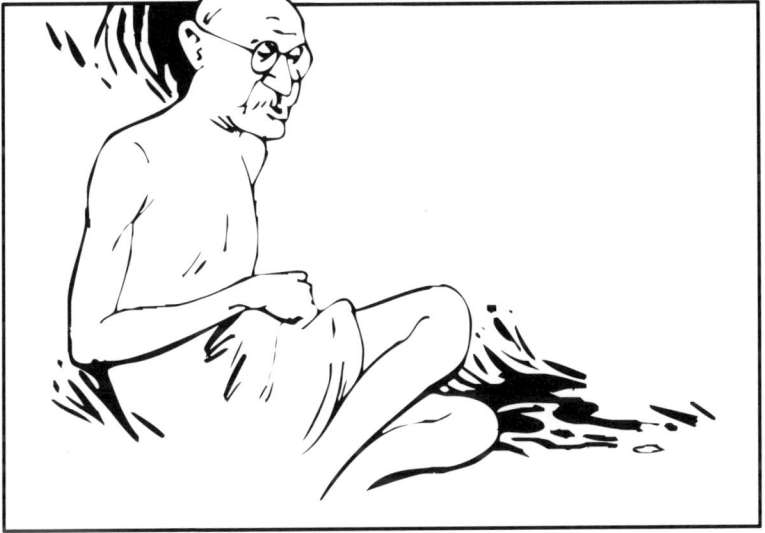

# On Matters Religious

THE seeker after Truth should be humbler than the dust. The world crushes the dust under its feet, but the seeker after truth should be so humble himself that even the dust could crush him. Only then, and not till then, will he have a glimpse of Truth. The dialogue between Vasishtha and Vishvamitra makes this abundantly clear. Christianity and Islam also amply bear it out ...

... What may appear as truth to one person will often appear as untruth to another person. But that need not worry the seeker. Where there is honest effort, it will be realized that what appear to be different truths are like the countless and apparently different leaves of the same tree ... Truth is the right designation of God. Hence there is nothing wrong in every man following Truth according to his lights. Indeed, it is his duty to do so. Then if there is a mistake on the part of anyone so following the Truth, it will be automatically set right. For the quest of Truth involves *tapas*—self-suffering, sometimes even unto death. There can be no place in it for even a trace of self-interest. In such selfless search for Truth nobody can lose his bearings for long.

HE who waits for God fails to understand that he possesses Him. Believe that God and happiness are one, and put all your happiness in the present moment.

MAN is not all body but he is something infinitely higher. Of all the animal creation of God, man is the only animal who has been created in order that he may know his Maker. Man's aim in life is not therefore to add from day to day to his material prospects and to his material possessions, but his predominant calling is from day to day to come nearer his own Maker.

ALL the religions of the world, while they may differ in other respects, unitedly proclaim that nothing lives in this world but truth.

HIGH thinking is inconsistent with complicated material life based on high speed imposed by Mammon worship.

THERE is no cause for despondency for a man who has faith and resolution.

THERE is nothing that wastes the body like worry, and one who has faith in God should be ashamed to worry about anything whatsoever. It is a difficult rule no doubt, for the simple reason that faith in God for the majority of mankind is either an intellectual belief or a blind belief, a kind of superstitious fear of something indefinable. But to ensure absolute freedom from fear requires a living utter faith which is a plant of slow, almost unperceived growth and requires to be constantly watered by tears that accompany genuine prayer. They are the tears of a lover that cannot brook a moment's separation from the loved one, or of a penitent who knows that it is some trace of impurity that keeps him away from the loved one.

NUMBEROUS examples have convinced me that God ultimately saves him whose motive is pure.

MANKIND is notoriously too dense to read the signs that God sends from time to time. We require drums to be beaten in our ears, before we should wake from our trance and hear the warning and see that to lose oneself in all is the only way to find oneself.

THE divine guidance often comes when the horizon is blackest .

WHEN every hope is gone, 'when helpers fail and comforts flee,' I find that help arrives somehow, from I know not where. Supplication, worship, prayer are no superstitions; they are acts more real than the acts of eating, drinking, sitting or walking. It is no exaggeration to say that they alone are real, all else is unreal.

PRAYER is the very essence and soul of religion, and therefore prayer must be the very core of the life of man, for no man can live without religion.

PRAYER is not asking. It is a longing of the soul.

PRAYER is not an old woman's idle amusement. Properly understood and applied, it is the most potent instrument of action.

GOD can never be realized by one who is not pure of heart. Self-purification therefore must mean purification in all walks of life ... But the path of self-purification is hard and steep. To attain to perfect purity one has to become absolutely passion free in thought, speech and action; to rise above the opposing currents of love and hatred, attachment and repulsion. I know that I have not in me as yet that triple purity, in spite of constant ceaseless striving for it. That is why the world's praise fails to move me, indeed it often stings me. To conquer the subtle passions seems to me far harder than the conquest of the world by force of arms. Ever since my return to India I have had the experience of the dormant passions lying within me. The knowledge of them has made me feel humiliated though not defeated. The experiences and experiments have sustained me and given me great joy. But I know that I still have before me a difficult path to traverse. I must reduce myself to zero. So long as a man does not of his own free will put himself last among his fellow creatures, there is no salvation for him.

GOD's grace never descends upon a man who is a slave to lust.

A TRULY religious person becomes a citizen of the world, but the service of one's own country is the stepping-stone to the service of humanity. And where service is rendered to the country consistently with the welfare of the world, it finally leads to self-realization.

HAD He made any distinctions of high and low between man and man, they would have been visible as are the distinctions between, say, an elephant and an ant. But He has endowed all human beings impartially with the same shape and the same natural wants.

WE are all His creatures; and just as in the eyes of parents all their children are absolutely equal, so also in God's eyes all His creatures must be equal.

WE are all tarred with the same brush, and are children of one and the same Creator, and as such the divine powers within us are infinite. To slight a single human being is to slight those divine powers, and thus to harm not only that being but with him the whole world.

THERE is no one without faults, not even men of God. They are men of God not because they are faultless, but because they know their own faults, they strive against them, they do not hide them and are ever ready to correct themselves.

HUMILITY should make the possessor realize that he is as nothing. Directly one imagines oneself to be something, there is egotism. If a man who keeps observances is proud of keeping them then he will lose much if not all of their value. And a man who is proud of his virtue often becomes a curse to his society. Society will not appreciate it, and he himself will fail to reap any benefit from it. Only a little thought will suffice to convince us that all creatures are nothing more than a mere atom in this universe. Our existence as embodied beings is purely momentary; what are a hundred years in eternity? But if we shatter the chains of egotism, and melt into the ocean of humanity, we share its dignity. To feel that we are something is to set up a barrier between God and ourselves; to cease feeling that we are something is to become one with God. A drop in the ocean partakes of the greatness of its parent, although it is unconscious of it, but it is dried up as soon as it enters upon an existence independent of the ocean. We do not exaggerate when we say that life on earth is a mere bubble.

NO one has that capacity to judge God. We are all drops in that limitless ocean of mercy.

PROVIDENCE has its appointed hour for everything. We cannot command results; we can only strive.

THERE never can be any conflict between the real interest of one's country and that of one's religion. Where there appears to be any, there is something wrong with one's religion; i.e. one's morals. True religion means good thought and good conduct. True patriotism also means good thought and good conduct. To set up a comparison between the two synonymous things is wrong.

I REJECT any religious doctrine that does not appeal to reason and is in conflict with morality.

TO see the all-pervading Spirit of Truth face to face, one must be able to love the meanest of creation as oneself. And a man who aspires after that cannot afford to keep out of any field of life. That is why my devotion to Truth has drawn me into the field of politics; and I can say without the slightest hesitation, and in all humility, that those who say that religion has nothing to do with politics do not know what religion means.

THE voice of the people is the voice of God.

GOD himself dare not appear to a hungry man, except in the form of bread.

'DO not worry in the least about yourself, leave all worry to God' — this appears to be the commandment in all religions. This need not frighten anyone. He who devotes himself to service with a clear conscience will day by day grasp the necessity for it in greater measure and will continually grow richer in faith. The path of service can hardly be trodden by one who is not prepared to renounce self-interest, and to recognize the conditions of his birth. Consciously or unconsciously, every one of us does render some service or other. If we cultivate the habit of doing this service deliberately, our desire for service will steadily grow stronger, and will make not only for our own happiness but that of the world at large.

CALL it then by whatever name you like, that which gives one the greatest solace in the midst of the severest fire is God.

IT is the quality of our work which will please God and not the quantity.

ONE'S faith has got to be bright and intelligent before it can enkindle faith in others.

FAITH is the function of the heart. It must be enforced by reason. The two are not antagonistic as some think. The more intense one's faith is, the more it whets one's reason. When faith becomes blind, it dies.

IT is a poor faith that needs fair weather for standing firm. That alone is true faith that stands the foulest weather.

IT is for us to make the effort. The result is always in God's hands.

OUR scriptures tell us that childhood, old age and death are incidents only to this perishable body of ours, and that man's spirit is eternal and immortal. That being so, why should we fear death? And where there is no fear of death, there can be no sorrow over it, either. Fear of death makes us devoid both of valour and religion, for want of valour is want of religious faith.

MAN'S ultimate aim is the realization of God, and all his activities - social, political, religious - have to be guided by the ultimate aim of the vision of God. The immediate service of all human beings becomes a necessary part of the endeavour because the only way to find God is to see Him in his creation and be one with it.

IN the divine account books only our actions are noted, not what we have read or what we have spoken.

ALL sins are committed in secrecy. The moment we realize that God witnesses even our thoughts, we shall be free.

SUBMISSION to convention in trivial matters in which there is no danger of deceiving others or oneself is often desirable and even necessary. But submission in matters of religion, especially where there is a positive repugnance from within and a danger of deceiving our neighbours and ourselves, cannot but be debasing.

NO religion which is narrow and cannot satisfy the test of reason will survive the coming reconstruction of society in which the values will have changed and character, not possession of wealth, title or birth, will be the test of merit.

WHAT is readily yielded to courtesy is never yielded to force. Submission to a courteous request is religion, submission to force is irreligion.

HINDUISM believes in the oneness of not merely all human life, but in the oneness of all that lives.

HINDUISM is the most tolerant of all religions.

IT some people, for their inward satisfaction and growth, change their religion, let them do so. I am, then, not against conversion. But I am against the modern methods of it. Conversion, nowadays, has become a matter of business, like any other.

JESUS, a man who was completely innocent, offered himself up as a sacrifice for the good of others, including his enemies, and became the ransom of the world. It was a perfect act.

IT was more than I could believe that Jesus was the only incarnate son of God, and that only he who believed in him would have everlasting life. If God could have sons, all of us were His sons. If Jesus was like a God, or God Himself, then all men were like God and could be God Himself. My reason was not ready to believe literally that Jesus by his death and by his blood redeemed the sins of the world ... I could accept Jesus as a martyr, an embodiment of sacrifice, and a divine teacher, but not as the most perfect man ever born. His death on the Cross was a great example to the world, but that there was anything like a mysterious or miraculous virtue in it, my heart could not accept ...

Philosophically there was nothing extraordinary in Christian principles. From the point of view of sacrifice, it seemed to me that the Hindus greatly surpassed the Christians. It was impossible for me to regard Christianity as a perfect religion or the greatest of all religions.

Thus if I could not accept Christianity either as a perfect, or the greatest religion, neither was I then convinced of Hinduism being such. Hindu defects were pressingly visible to me.

... I COULD not possibly read through the Old Testament. I invariably went to sleep. I read the book of Genesis, and the chapters that followed invariably sent me to sleep. But just for the sake of being able to say that I had read it, I plodded through the other books with much difficulty and without the least interest or understanding. I disliked reading the book of Numbers.

But the New Testament produced a different impression, especially The Sermon on the Mount which went straight to my heart. I compared it with the *Gita*. The verses, 'But I say unto you, that ye resist not evil: but whosoever smite thee on the right cheek, turn to him the other also. And if any man take away thy coat let him have thy cloak too,' delighted me beyond measure and put me in mind of Shamal Bhatt's 'For a bowl of water, give a goodly meal.' My young mind tried to unify the teaching of the *Gita*, *The Light of Asia* and the Sermon on the Mount. That renunciation was the highest form of religion appealed to me greatly.

ALL your scholarship, all your study of the scriptures will be in vain if you fail to translate their teachings into your daily life.

AS soon as we lose the moral basis, we cease to be religious. There is no such thing as religion overriding morality. Man, for instance, cannot be untruthful, cruel or incontinent and claim to have God on his side.

IT is easy enough to be friendly to one's friends. But to befriend the one who regards himself as your enemy is the quintessence of true religion. The other is mere business.

# On Virtue and Morality

I WILL give you a talisman. Whenever you are in doubt or when the self becomes too much with you, try the following expedient: Recall the face of the poorest and the most helpless man whom you may have seen and ask yourself if the step you contemplate is going to be of any use to him. Will he be able to gain anything by it? Will it restore him to control over his own life and destiny? ... Then you will find your doubts and your self melting away.

SERVICE without humility is selfishness and egotism.

ONE who would serve will not waste a thought upon his own comforts, which he leaves to be attended or neglected by his Master on high. He will not, therefore, encumber himself with everything that comes his way; he will take only what he strictly needs and leave the rest. He will be calm, free from anger and unruffled in mind even if he finds himself inconvenienced. His service, like virtue, is its own reward, and he will rest content with it.

JUST as one must not receive, so must one not possess anything one does not really need. It would be a breach of this principle to possess unnecessary foodstuffs, clothing, or furniture. For instance, one must not keep a chair if one can do without it. In observing this principle one is led to a progressive simplification of one's own life.

RICHES are no test of goodness. Indeed, poverty is the only test. A good man voluntarily embraces poverty.

THERE comes a time when an individual becomes irresistible and his action becomes all pervasive in effect. This comes when he reduces himself to zero.

TO enjoy life, one should give up the lure of life.

THE main purpose of life is to live rightly, think rightly, act rightly; the soul must languish when we give all our thoughts to the body.

ONE man cannot do right in one department of his life whilst he is occupied in doing wrong in another department. Life is one indivisible whole.

MAN has reason, discrimination and free will such as it is. The brute has no such thing. It is not a free agent, and knows no such distinction between virtue and vice, good and evil. Man, being a free agent, knows these distinctions and, when he follows his higher nature, shows himself far superior to the brute. But when he follows his baser nature, he can show himself lower than the brute.

MAN'S destined purpose is to conquer old habits, to overcome the evil in him and to restore good to its rightful place.

WE cannot, in a moment, get rid of the habits of a lifetime.

A MAN must arrange his physical and cultural circumstances so that they do not hinder him in his service of humanity, on which all his energies should be concentrated.

WE must gladly give up custom that is against reason, justice and religion of the heart. We must not ignorantly cling to bad custom and part with it when we must, like a miser parting with his ill-gotten hoard out of pressure and expediency.

EACH one has to find his peace from within. And peace to be real must be unaffected by outside circumstances.

ALWAYS aim at complete harmony of thought and word and deed. Always aim at purifying your thoughts and everything will be well. There is nothing more potent than thought. Deed follows word and word follows thought. The word is the result of a mighty thought, and where the thought is mighty and pure, the result is always mighty and pure.

CONTROL over thought is a long, painful and laborious process. But I am convinced that no time, no labour and no pain is too much for the glorious result to be achieved.

COMPLETE extinction of impure thought is impossible without ceaseless penance. There is only one way to achieve this. The moment an impure thought arises, confront it with a pure one. This is possible only with God's grace and God's grace comes with ceaseless communion with Him and complete self-surrender.

HIDE not your thoughts. If it is shameful to reveal them, it is more shameful to think them.

PURITY consists first of all in possessing a pure heart, but what there is in the heart comes out also and is shown in outward acts and outward behaviour.

THE first step in self-restraint is restraint of the thoughts.

A MAN who broods on evil is as bad as a man who does evil.

THE mind may wander, but let not the senses wander.

IF the senses wander where the mind takes them, one is done for. But he who keeps control over the physical senses will some day be able to bring impure thoughts under control.

NOT to have control over the senses is like sailing in a rudderless ship, bound to break to pieces on coming in contact with the very first rock.

ABOVE all keep yourselves pure and clean, and learn to keep your promises even at the cost of your life. Breach of promise is a base surrender of truth.

PERSONALLY I hold that a man who deliberately and intelligently takes a pledge and then breaks it, forfeits his manhood. And just as a copper coin treated with mercury not only becomes valueless when found out but also makes its owner liable to punishment, in the same way a man who lightly pledges his word and then breaks it becomes a man of straw and fits himself for punishment here as well as hereafter.

A VOW is a fixed and unalterable determination to do a thing, when such a determination is related to something noble which can only uplift the man who makes the resolve. A vow is to all other indifferent resolves what a right angle is to all other angles. And just as a right angle gives an unvarying and correct measure, so does a man of vows that are rightly followed give of himself an unvariable and correct measure.

THE world, though not itself virtuous, pays an unconscious homage to virtue.

THERE are no two opinions about the fact that intellect rather than riches will lead. It might equally be admitted that the heart rather than the intellect will eventually lead. Character, not brain, will count at the crucial moment.

TRUTH resides in every human heart, and one has to search for it there, and to be guided by truth as one sees it. But no one has a right to coerce others to act according to his own view of truth.

IT is good to see ourselves as others see us. Try as we may, we are never able to know ourselves fully as we are, especially the evil side of us. This we can only do if we are not angry with our critics, but will take in good heart whatever they might have to say.

IT is not our differences that matter. It is the meanness behind them that is ugly.

OUR besetting sin is not difference, but our littleness.

THERE is a higher court than courts of justice and that is the court of conscience. It supersedes all other courts.

IN matters of conscience, the law of the majority has no place.

IT is unwise to be sure of one's own wisdom. It is healthy to be reminded that the strongest might weaken and the wisest might err.

THOSE who want to be good are not in a hurry. They know that to impregnate people with good takes a long time.

MAN often becomes what he believes himself to be. If I keep on saying to myself that I cannot do a certain thing, it is possible that I may end by really becoming incapable of doing it. On the contrary, if I have the belief that I can do it, I shall surely acquire the capacity to do it, even if I may not have it at the beginning.

MANLINESS consists in making circumstances subserve to ourselves. Those who will not heed themselves perish. To understand this principle is not to be impatient, not to reproach fate, not to blame others. He who understands the doctrine of self-help blames himself for failure.

MANLINESS consists not in bluff, bravado or lordliness. It consists in daring to do the right and facing the consequences, whether it is in matters social, political or other. It consists in deeds, not in words.

IN fact the right to perform one's duties is the only right that is worth living for and dying for. It covers all legitimate rights.

SELF-HELP is the capacity to stand on one's legs without anybody's help. This does not mean indifference to or rejection of outside help, but it means the capacity to be at peace with oneself, to preserve one's self-respect, when outside help is not forthcoming or is refused.

INDEED, one's faith in one's plans and methods is fully tested when the horizon before one is the blackest.

DIGNITY of the soul and self-respect are interpreted differently by different persons. I am aware that self-respect is often misinterpreted. The over-sensitive man may see disrespect or hurt in almost everything. Such a man does not really understand what self-respect is.

A HUMBLE person is not himself conscious of his humility. Truth and the like perhaps admit of measurement, but not humility. Inborn humility can never remain hidden, and yet the possessor is unaware of its existence.

IT is my firm belief that love sustains the earth. There only is life where there is love. Life without love is death. Love is the reverse of the coin of which the obverse is Truth.

LOVE never claims, it ever gives. Love ever suffers, never resents, never revenges itself.

A COWARD is incapable of love; it is the prerogative of the brave.

BRAVERY is not a quality of the body, it is of the soul. I have seen cowards encased in tough muscle, and rare courage in the frailest body.

FEAR has its use, but cowardice has none. I may not put my fingers into the jaws of a snake, but the very sight of the snake need not strike terror into me. The trouble is that we often die many times before death overtakes us.

WHY worry over a thing that is inevitable? Why die before death?

TO be afraid of dying is like being afraid of discarding an old worn out garment.

IT is because we fear death so much for ourselves that we shed tears over the death of others.

THE will to live is not irrational. It is also natural. Attachment to life is not a delusion. It is very real. Above all, life has a purpose. To seek to defeat that purpose is a sin. Therefore suicide is very rightly held to be a sin.

THERE are some actions from which escape is a godsend, both for the man who escapes and those about him. Man, as soon as he gets back his consciousness of what is right, is thankful to the Divine mercy for the escape. As we know that a man often succumbs to temptation however much he may resist it, we also know that Providence often intercedes and saves him in spite of himself. How all this happens, how far a man is free and how far a creature of circumstances, how far free will comes into play and where fate enters on the scene, all this is a mystery and will remain a mystery.

TIME is a merciless enemy, as it is also a merciful friend and healer.

TRUE friendship is an identity of souls rarely to be found in this world. Only between like natures can friendship be altogether worthy and enduring. Friends react on one another. Hence in friendship there is little hope for reform. I am of the opinion that all exclusive intimacies are to be avoided, for man takes in vice far more readily than virtue. And he who would be friend with God must remain alone, or make the whole world his friend.

NOT mad rush, but unperturbed calmness brings wisdom. This maxim holds as true today as when it was first propounded ages ago.

WISDOM is no monopoly of one continent or race.

MUST I do all the evil I can before I learn to shun it? Is it not enough to know the evil to shun it? If not, we should be sincere enough to admit that we love evil too well to give it up.

THREE fourths of the miseries and misunderstandings in the world will disappear if we step into the shoes of our adversaries and understand their standpoint. We will then agree with our adversaries or think of them charitably.

IT is wrong, it is sinful, to consider some people lower than ourselves.

THERE will never be real equality so long as one feels inferior or superior to the other.

IT can never be an act of merit to look down upon any human being as inferior to us.

ANGER and intolerance are the twin enemies of correct understanding.

ANGER is a sort of madness and the noblest causes have been damaged by advocates affected with temporary lunacy.

TO trust is a virtue. It is weakness that begets distrust

THE moment there is suspicion about a person's motives everything he does becomes tainted.

FAITH knows no disappointment.

MONOTONY is the law of nature. Look at the monotonous manner in which the sun rises. And imagine the catastrophe that would befall the universe if the sun became capricious and went in for a variety of pastimes. But there is a monotony that sustains and a monotony that kills. The monotony of necessary occupation is exhilarating and life giving. An artist never tires of his art. A spinner who has mastered his art will certainly be able to do sustained work without fatigue. There is a music about the spindle which the practised spinner catches without fail.

NO sacrifice is worth the name unless it is a joy. Sacrifice and a long face go ill together. Sacrifice is 'making sacred'. He must be a poor specimen of humanity who is in need of sympathy for his sacrifice.

THAT sacrifice which causes pain loses its sacred character and will break down under stress. One gives up things that one considers to be injurious and therefore there should be pleasure attendant upon the giving up.

THE mice which helplessly find themselves between the cat's teeth acquire no merit from their enforced sacrifice.

PERSEVERANCE opens up treasures which bring perennial joy.

IT is health which is real wealth and not pieces of gold and silver.

INCREASE of material comforts, it may be generally laid down, does not in any way whatsoever conduce to moral growth.

THERE is sufficiency in the world for man's needs but not for man's greed.

IT is my certain conviction that no man loses his freedom except through his own weakness.

WHEN a slave begins to take pride in his fetters and hugs them like precious ornaments, the triumph of the slave owner is complete.

ALL crime is a kind of disease and should be treated as such.

CRIME and vice generally require darkness for prowling. They disappear when light plays upon them.

INSTEAD of being angry with the thief, you take pity on him. You think that this stealing must be a disease with him.

Henceforth, therefore, you keep your doors and windows open, you change your sleeping place, and you keep things in a manner most accessible to him. The robber comes again and is confused as all this is new to him; nevertheless, he takes away your things. But his mind is agitated. He inquires about you in the village, he comes to learn about your broad and loving heart, he repents, he begs your pardon, returns you your things and leaves off the stealing habit. He becomes your servant and you find for him honourable employment.

A CLEAN confession combined with a promise never to commit the sin again, when offered before one who has the right to receive it, is the purest type of repentance.

HATE the sin and love the sinner.

ONE may detest the wickedness of a brother without hating him.

HAVE I not told you times without number, that ultimately a deceiver only deceives himself?

TO err is human and it must be held to be equally human to forgive, if we, though being fallible, would like to be forgiven rather than punished and reminded of our deeds.

TO forgive is not to forget. The merit lies in loving in spite of the vivid knowledge that the one that must be loved is not a friend. There is no merit in loving an enemy when you forget him for a friend.

THE weak can never forgive. Forgiveness is the attribute of the strong.

IF the beasts had intelligent speech at their command, they would state a case against man that would stagger humanity.

IT is my firm conviction that all good action is bound to bear fruit in the end.

MORALITY is the basis of all things and truth is the substance of morality.

WE cease to grow the moment we cease to distinguish between virtue and vice.

PANIC is the most demoralising state anyone can be in. There never is any cause for panic. One must keep heart whatever happens. War is an unmitigated evil. But it certainly does one good thing. It drives away fear and brings bravery to the surface.

THE appeal of reason is more to the head but the penetration of the heart comes from suffering. It opens up the inner understanding in man.

SUFFERING is the badge of the human race, not the sword.

LIFE is but an endless series of experiments.

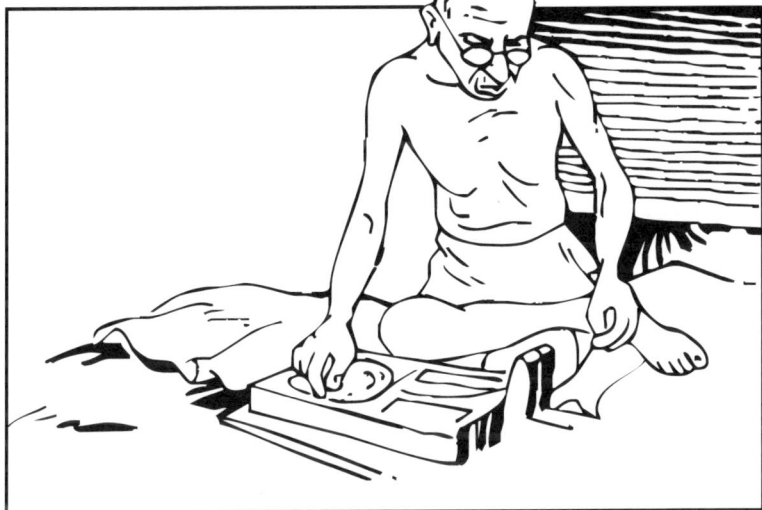

# On Society

IT is difficult but not impossible to conduct strictly honest business. What is true is that honesty is incompatible with amassing a large fortune.

'IT is easier for a camel to go through the eye of a needle than for a rich man to enter the Kingdom of God!' Here you have an eternal rule of life stated in the noblest words the English language is capable of producing. But the disciples showed unbelief as we do even to this day. And Jesus said: 'Verily I say unto you that there is no man that has left house or brethren or sisters, or father or mother, or wife or child or lands for my sake and the Gospels, but he shall receive one hundred fold.' I hold that economic progress is antagonistic to real progress. Hence the ancient ideal has been the limitation of activities promoting wealth. This does not put an end to all material ambition. We should still have, as we always have had, in our midst people who make the pursuit of wealth their aim in life. But we have always recognized that it is a fall from the ideal. It's a beautiful thing to know that the wealthiest among us have often felt that to have remained voluntarily poor would have been a higher state for them.

I MUST confess that I do not draw a sharp or any distinction between economics and ethics. Economics that hurt the moral well being of an individual or a nation are immoral and therefore sinful. Thus the economics that permit one country to prey upon another are immoral. It is sinful to eat American wheat and let my neighbour, the grain dealer, starve for want of custom.

THE distinguishing characteristic of modern civilization is an indefinite multiplicity of human wants. The characteristic of ancient civilization is an imperative restriction upon, and a strict regulating of, these wants.

CIVILIZATION, in the real sense of the term, consists not in the multiplication, but in the deliberate and voluntary reduction of human wants. This alone promotes real happiness and contentment, and increases the capacity for service.

CIVILIZATION is the encouragement of differences. Civilization thus becomes a synonym of democracy. Force, violence, pressure, or compulsion with a view to conformity, is both uncivilized and undemocratic.

WE get the government we deserve. When we improve, the government is also bound to improve.

MY notion of democracy is that under it the weakest should have the same opportunity as the strongest. This can never happen except through nonviolence.

GOOD government is no substitute for self-government.

THE history of the world is full of men who rose to leadership by sheer force of self-confidence, bravery and tenacity.

PERFORMANCE of one's duty should be independent of public opinion. I have all along held that one is bound to act according to what appears to one to be right, even though it may appear to others to be wrong. And experience has shown that that is the only correct course. I admit that there is always the possibility of one's mistaking right for wrong and vice-versa, but often one learns to recognize wrong only through unconscious error. On the other hand, if a man fails to follow the light from within for fear of public opinion or any other similar reason, he would never be able to know right from wrong and in the end lose all distinction between the two.

A LEADER is useless when he acts against the promptings of his own conscience.

THE acts of men who have come out to serve or lead have always been misunderstood since the beginning of the world and none can help it.

TO put up with all these misrepresentations and to stick to one's guns come what might; this is the essence of true leadership.

HEALTHY, well informed, balanced criticism is the ozone of public life. A most democratic minister is likely to go wrong without ceaseless watch from the public.

POURING ridicule on one's opponent is an approved method in 'civilized politics'.

CRITICISM of public men is a welcome sign of public awakening. It keeps workers on the alert.

HONEST differences are often a sign of progress.

PUBLIC opinion alone can keep a society pure and healthy.

CONSTANT development is the law of life, and a man who always tries to maintain his dogmas in order to appear consistent drives himself into a false position.

BLIND adoration is often embarrassing and equally often painful.

RIGHTS accrue automatically to him who performs his duties.

THE true source of rights is duty. If we discharge all our duties, rights will not be far to seek.

IF the individual ceases to count, what is left of society? Individual freedom alone can make a man voluntarily surrender himself completely to the service of society. If it is wrested from him, he becomes an automaton and society is ruined. No society can possibly be built on a denial of individual freedom. It is contrary to the very nature of man. Just as a man will not grow horns or a tail, so he will not exist as a man if he has no mind of his own. In reality, even those who do not believe in the liberty of the individual believe in their nature.

CLASSLESS society is the ideal not merely to be aimed at but to be worked for.

A MAN cannot develop his mind by simply writing and reading or making speeches all day.

I AM no indiscriminate worshipper of all that goes under the name of 'ancient'. I have never hesitated to demolish all that is evil or immoral, but with that reservation I must confess to you that I am an adorer of ancient institutions, and it hurts me to think that people in their rush for everything modern despise all their ancient traditions and ignore them in their lives.

A FLAG is a necessity for all nations. Millions have died for it.

IT *(a flag)* is no doubt a kind of idolatry which it would be a sin to destroy. For a flag represents an ideal. The unfurling of the Union Jack evokes in the English breast sentiments whose strengths it is difficult to measure. The Stars and Stripes means the world to the Americans. The Star and Crescent will call forth the best bravery in Islam.

THE sole aim of journalism should be service. The press is a great power, but just as an unchained torrent of water submerges the whole countryside and devastates crops, even so an uncontrolled pen serves but to destroy. If the control is from without, it proves more poisonous than want of control.

It can be profitable only when exercised from within. If this line of reasoning is correct, how many journals in the world would stand the test? But who would stop those that are useless? And who should be the judge? The useful and the useless must, like good and evil generally, go on together and man must make his choice.

WHO can deny that much that passes for science and art today destroys the soul instead of uplifting it and instead of evoking the best in us, panders to our basest passions?

FOR years man dreamed of freeing the energy stored in the atom. Hardly has he realized his dream than he begins to groan at its danger: were we then so naive as to think we were going to play with harmless toys right to the end?

# On Education

I DID not believe in the existing system of education, and I had a mind to find out by experience and experiment the true system. Only this much I knew - that, under ideal conditions, true education could only be imparted by the parents, and then there should be a minimum of outside help ...

THERE is no school equal to a decent home and no teachers equal to honest, virtuous parents.

I HAVE always felt that the true text book for the pupil is his teacher. I remember very little that my teachers taught me from books, but I have even now a clear recollection of the things they taught me independently of books.

Children take in much more and with less labour through their ears than through their eyes. I do not remember having read any book from cover to cover with my boys. But I gave them, in my own language, all that I had digested from my reading of various books, and I dare say they are still carrying a recollection of it in their minds. It was laborious for them to remember what they learnt from books, but what I imparted to them by word of mouth, they could repeat with the greatest ease. Reading was a task for them, but listening to me was a pleasure, when I did not bore them by failing to make my subject interesting. And from the questions that my talks prompted them to put, I had a measure of their power of understanding.

IT is for teachers to make attractive and intelligible what to pupils may at first appear repulsive or uninteresting.

IT is a gross superstition to suppose that knowledge can only be obtained by going to schools and colleges. The world produced brilliant students before schools and colleges came into being. There is nothing so ennobling or lasting as self-study. Schools and colleges make most of us mere receptacles for holding the superfluities of knowledge. Wheat is left out and more husk is taken in.

TO develop the spirit is to build character and to enable one to work towards a knowledge of God and self-realization. And I held that this was an essential part of the training of the young, and that all training without culture of the spirit was of no use, and might even be harmful.

I am familiar with the superstition that self-realization is possible only in the fourth stage of life, i.e., *sannyasa* (renunciation). But it is a matter of common knowledge that those who defer preparation for this invaluable experience until the last stage of life attain not self-realization but old age, amounting to a second pitiable childhood, living as a burden on this earth ...

How then was this spiritual training to be given? I made the children memorize and recite hymns, and read to them from books on moral training. But that was far from satisfying. As I came into closer contact with them I saw that it was not through books that one could impart training of the spirit. Just as physical training was to be imparted through physical exercise, and intellectual through intellectual exercise, even so the training of the spirit was possible only through the exercise of the spirit. All the exercise of the spirit entirely depended on the life and character of the teacher. The teacher had always to be mindful of his p's and q's, whether he was in the midst of his boys or not.

It is possible for a teacher situated miles away to affect the spirit of the pupils by his way of living. It would be idle for me, if I were a liar, to teach boys to tell the truth. A cowardly teacher would never succeed in making his boys valiant, and a stranger to self-restraint could never teach his pupils the value of self-restraint. I saw, therefore, that I must be an eternal object lesson to the boys and girls living with me. They thus became my teachers, and I learnt I must be good and live straight, if only for their sakes.

A CHILVALROUS boy would always keep his mind pure, his eyes straight, and his hands unpolluted. You do not need to go to any school to learn these fundamental maxims of life, and if you have this triple character, you will build on a solid foundation.

ALL your scholarship, all your study of Shakespeare and Wordsworth would be in vain if at the same time you do not build your character, and attain mastery over your thoughts and actions. When you have attained self-mastery and learnt to control your passions, you will not utter notes of despair. You cannot give your hearts and profess poverty of action. To give one's heart is to give all. You must, to start with, have hearts to give. And this you can do if you will cultivate them.

IT is knowledge that ultimately gives salvation.

WE labour under a superstition that the child has nothing to learn during the first five years of its life. On the contrary, the fact is that the child never learns in later life what it learns in its first five years. The education of the child begins with conception.

CHILDREN inherit the qualities of the parents no less than their physical features. Environment does play an important part, but the original capital on which a child starts in life is inherited from its ancestors. I have also seen children successfully surmounting the effects of an evil inheritance. That is due to purity being an inherent attribute of the soul.

PURITY of personal life is the one indispensable condition for building up the education of the soul.

I HAVE always been opposed to corporal punishment. I remember only one occasion on which I physically punished one of my sons. I have therefore never to this day been able to decide whether I was right or wrong in using the ruler. Probably it was improper, for it was prompted by anger and a desire to punish. Had it been an expression only of my distress, I should have considered it justified.

THE student's mind must not be caged, nor for that matter those of the teachers.

DAY by day it became increasingly clear to me how very

difficult it was to bring up and educate boys and girls in the right way. If I was to be their real teacher and guardian, I must touch their hearts. I must share their joys and sorrows, I must help them to solve the problems that faced them, and I must take along the right channel the surging aspirations of their youth ... Once when I was in Johannesburg I received tidings of the moral fall of two of the inmates of the Ashram. News of an apparent failure or reverse in the *satyagraha* struggle would not have shocked me, but this news came upon me like a thunderbolt. The same day I took the train for Phoenix. Mr. Kallenbach insisted on accompanying me. He had noticed the state I was in. He would not brook the thought of my going alone, for he happened to be the bearer of the tidings which had so upset me.

During the journey my duty seemed clear to me. I felt that the guardian or teacher was responsible, to some extent at least, for the lapse of his ward or pupil. So my responsibility regarding the incident in question became clear to me as daylight. My wife had already warned me in the matter, but being of a trusting nature, I had ignored her caution. I felt that the only way the guilty parties could be made to realize my distress and the depth of their own fall would be for me to do some penance. So I imposed upon myself a fast for seven days and a vow to have only one meal a day for a period of four months and a half. Mr. Kallenbach tried to dissuade me, but in vain ...

I felt greatly relieved, for the decision meant a heavy load off my mind. The anger against the guilty parties subsided and gave place to the purest pity for them. Thus considerably eased, I reached the ashram at Phoenix. I made further investigation and acquainted myself with some more details I needed to know.

My penance pained everybody, but it cleared the atmosphere. Everyone came to realize what a terrible thing it was to be sinful, and the bond that bound me to the boys and girls became stronger ...

THERE is no question about the teacher's responsibility for the errors of his pupil.

IF good children are taught together with bad ones and thrown into their company, they will lose nothing, provided the experiment is conducted under the watchful care of their parents and guardians. Children wrapped up in cottonwool are not always proof against all temptation or contamination. It is true, however, that when boys and girls of all kinds of upbringing are kept and taught together, the parents and the teachers are put to the severest test. They have constantly to be on the alert.

I HOLD it quite wrong on the part of students and pupils to take part in political demonstrations and party politics. Such ferment interferes with serious study and unfits students for solid work as future citizens.

A STUDENT, no matter how old or wise he is, surrenders when he joins a school or college, the right of rejecting its discipline.

# On Ahimsa

MAN and his deed are two distinct things. Whereas a good deed should call forth approbation and a wicked deed disapprobation, the doer of the deed, whether good or wicked, always deserves respect or pity, as the case may be. 'Hate the sin and not the sinner' is a precept which, though easy enough to understand, is rarely practised, and that is why the poison of hatred spreads in the world.

THIS *ahimsa is* the very basis of the search for truth. I am realizing every day that the search is in vain unless it is founded on *ahimsa* as the basis. It is quite proper to resist and attack a system, but to resist and attack its author is tantamount to resisting and attacking oneself. For we are all tarred with the same brush, and are children of one and the same Creator, and as such the divine powers within us are infinite. To slight a single human being is to slight those divine powers, and thus to harm not only that being, but with him the whole world.

AHIMSA is a comprehensive principle. We are helpless mortals caught in the conflagration of *himsa*. The saying that life lives on life has a deep meaning in it. Man cannot for a moment live without consciously or unconsciously committing outward *himsa*. The very fact of his living — eating, drinking and moving about — necessarily involves some *himsa*, destruction of life, be it ever so minute. A votary of *ahimsa* therefore remains true to his faith if the spring of all his actions is compassion, if he shuns to the best of his ability the destruction of the tiniest creature, tries to save it, and thus incessantly strives to be free from the deadly coil of *himsa*. He will be constantly growing in self-restraint and compassion, but he can never become entirely free from outward *himsa*.

Then again, because underlying *ahimsa* is the unity of all life, the error of one cannot but effect all, and hence man cannot be wholly free from *himsa*. So long as he continues to be a social being, he cannot but participate in the *himsa* that the very existence of society involves. When two nations are fighting, the duty of a votary of *ahimsa* is to stop the war. He who is not equal to that duty, he who has no power of resisting war, he who is not qualified to resist war, may take part in the war, and yet wholeheartedly try to free himself, his nation and the world from war.

AHIMSA and truth are so intertwined that it is practically impossible to disentangle and separate them. They are like the two sides of a coin, or rather a smooth unstamped metal disc. Who can say which is the obverse and which the reverse? Nevertheless, *ahimsa* is the means; truth is the end. Means, to be means, must be always within our reach, and so *ahimsa* is our supreme duty. If we take care of the means, we are bound to reach the end sooner or later. When once we have grasped this point, final victory is beyond question. Whatever difficulties we encounter, whatever apparent reverse we sustain, we may not give up the quest for truth.

MY uniform experience has convinced me that there is no other God than truth ... and ... that the only means for the realization of truth is *ahimsa*.

AHIMSA is the attribute of the soul and is therefore to be practised by everybody in all the affairs of life. If it cannot be practised in all departments, it has no practical value.

... HOWEVER sincere my strivings after *ahimsa* have been, they have still been imperfect and inadequate. The little fleeting glimpses, therefore, that I have been able to have of truth can hardly convey an idea of the indescribable lustre of truth, a million times more intense than that of the sun we daily see with our eyes. In fact, what I have caught is only the faintest glimmer of that mighty effulgence. But this much I can say with assurance, as a result of all my experiments, that a perfect vision of truth can only follow a complete realization of *ahimsa*.

IDENTIFICATION with everything that lives is impossible without self-purification; without self-purification the observance of the law of *ahimsa* must remain an empty dream.

AHIMSA is the farthest limit of humility.

AHIMSA is not the crude thing it has been made to appear. Not to hurt any living thing is no doubt a part of *ahimsa*. But it is its least expression. The principle of *ahimsa* is hurt by every evil thought, by undue haste, by lying, by hatred, by wishing ill to anybody. It is also violated by our holding on to what the world needs.

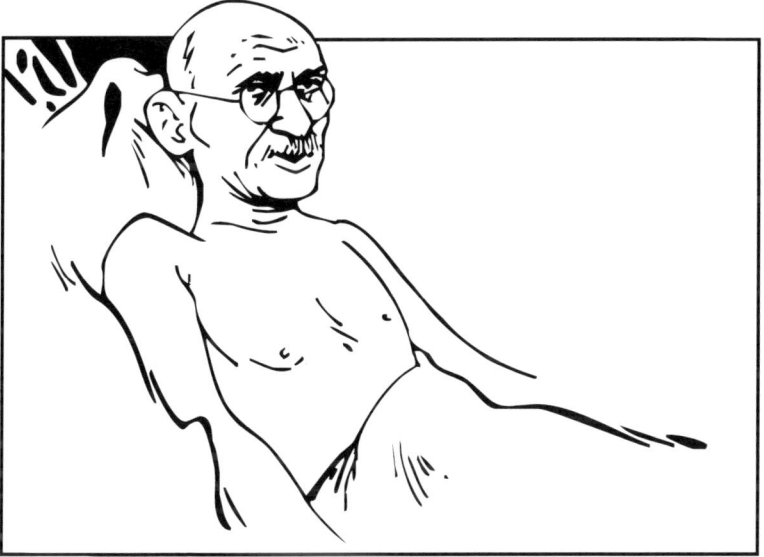

# On Satyagraha

THE term *satyagraha* was coined by me in order to distinguish it from the movement then going on under the name of 'Passive Resistance'. Its root meaning is 'holding on to truth', hence, 'force of righteousness'. I have also called it 'love force' or 'soul force'. In the application of *satyagraha* I discovered in the earliest stages that pursuit of truth did not permit violence being inflicted on one's opponent, but that he must be weaned away from error by patience and sympathy. For what appears truth to one may appear to be error for the other. And patience means self-suffering. So the doctrine came to mean vindication of truth, not by the infliction of suffering on the opponent, but on one's self.

THE principle called *satyagraha* came into being before that name was invented. Indeed when it was born, I myself could not say what it was. In Gujarati also we used the English phrase 'passive resistance' to describe it. When in a meeting of Europeans I found that the term 'passive resistance' was too narrowly construed, that it was supposed to be a weapon of the weak, that it could be characterized by hatred, and that it could finally manifest itself as violence, I had to demur to all these statements and explain the real nature of the Indian movement. It was clear that a new word must be coined by the Indians to designate their struggle.

But I could not for the life of me find out a new name, and therefore offered a nominal prize through *Indian Opinion* to the reader who made the best suggestion on the subject. As a result Maganlal Gandhi coined the word '*sadagraha*' (sat = truth, agraha = firmness) and won the prize. But in order to make it clearer I changed the word to '*satyagraha*' which has since become current in Gujarati as a designation for the struggle.

SATYAGRAHA is a force that may be used by individuals as well as by communities. It may be used in political as in domestic affairs. Its universal applicability is a demonstration of its permanence and invincibility. It can be used alike by men, women, and children.

SATYAGRAHA is gentle, it never wounds. It must not be the result of anger or malice. It is never fussy, never impatient, never vociferous. It is the direct opposite of compulsion. It was conceived as a complete substitute for violence.

BEFORE one can be fit for the practice of civil disobedience one must have rendered a willing and respectful obedience to the state laws. For the most part we obey such laws out of fear of the penalty of their breach, and this holds good particularly in respect of such laws as do not involve a moral principle. For instance, an honest, respectable man will not suddenly take to stealing, whether there is a law against stealing or not, but this very man will not feel any remorse for failure to observe the rule about carrying headlights on bicycles after dark. Indeed it is doubtful whether he would even accept advice kindly about being more careful in this respect. But he would observe any obligatory rule of this kind, if only to escape the inconvenience of facing prosecution for a breach of the rule. Such compliance is not, however, the willing and spontaneous obedience that is required of a *satyagrahi*. A *satyagrahi* obeys the laws of society intelligently and of his own free will, because he considers it to be his sacred duty to do so. It is only when a person has thus obeyed the laws of society scrupulously that he is in a position to judge as to which particular rules are good and just and which unjust and iniquitous. Only then does the right accrue to him of the civil disobedience of certain laws in well defined circumstances.

SATYAGRAHA is a force that works silently and apparently slowly. In reality, there is no force in the world that is so direct or so swift in working.

IN *satyagraha*, it is never the numbers that count; it is always the quality, more so when the forces of violence are uppermost. Then it is often forgotten that it is never the intention of the *satyagrahi* to embarrass the wrongdoer. The appeal is never to his fear; it is, must be, always to his heart. The *satyagrahi's* object is to convert, not to coerce the wrongdoer. He should avoid artificiality in all his doings. He acts naturally and from inward conviction.

THUS, whilst this movement for the preservation of nonviolence was making steady though slow progress on the one hand, the Government's policy of lawless repression was in full career on the other, and was manifesting itself in the Punjab in all its nakedness. Leaders were put under arrest;

martial law, which in other words meant no law, was proclaimed; special tribunals were set up. These tribunals were not courts of justice but instruments for carrying out the arbitrary will of the autocrat. Sentences were passed unwarranted by evidence and in flagrant violation of justice. In Amritsar innocent men and women were made to crawl like worms on their bellies. Before this outrage the Jalianwala tragedy paled into insignificance in my eyes, though it was this massacre principally that attracted the attention of the people of India and of the world.

I was pressed to proceed to the Punjab immediately in disregard of consequences. I wrote and also telegraphed to the Viceroy asking for permission to go there, but in vain. If I proceeded without the necessary permission, I should not be allowed to cross the boundary of the Punjab, but left to find what satisfaction I could from civil disobedience. I was thus confronted by a serious dilemma. As things stood, to break the order against my entry into the Punjab could, it seemed to me, hardly be classed as civil disobedience, for I did not see around me the kind of peaceful atmosphere that I wanted, and the unbridled repression in the Punjab had further served to aggravate and deepen the feelings of resentment. For me, therefore, to offer civil disobedience at such a time, even if it were possible, would have been like fanning the flame. I therefore decided not to proceed to the Punjab in spite of the suggestion of friends. It was a bitter pill for me to swallow. Tales of rank injustice and oppression came pouring in daily from the Punjab, but all I could do was to sit helplessly and gnash my teeth.

A SATYAGRAHI bids goodbye to fear. He is therefore never afraid of trusting the opponent. Even if the opponent plays him false twenty times, the *satyagrahi is* ready to trust him the twenty-first time, for an implicit trust in human nature is the very essence of his creed.

ALTHOUGH noncooperation is one of the main weapons in the armoury of *satyagraha*, it should not be forgotten that it is, after all, only a means to secure the cooperation of the opponent consistently with truth and justice ... Avoidance of all relationship with the opposing power, therefore, can never be a *satyagrahi's* object, but transformation or purification of that relationship.

THERE is no time limit for a *satyagrahi*, nor is there a limit to his capacity for suffering. Hence, there is no such thing as defeat in *satyagraha*.

MY experience has taught me that a law of progression applies to every righteous struggle. But in the case of *satyagraha*, the law amounts to an axiom. As a *satyagraha* struggle progresses onward, many other elements help to swell its current and there is a constant growth in the results to which it leads. This is really inevitable and is bound up with the first principles of *satyagraha.* For in *satyagraha* the minimum is also the maximum, there is no question of retreat and the only possible movement is an advance.

# On the Gita

TOWARDS the end of my second year in England I came across two Theosophists, brothers, and both unmarried. They talked to me about the *Gita*. They were reading Sir Edwin Arnold's translation, *The Song Celestial*, and they invited me to read the original with them. I felt ashamed, as I had read the divine poem neither in Sanskrit nor in Gujarati. I was constrained to tell them that I had not read the *Gita*, but that I would gladly read it with them, and that though my knowledge of Sanskrit was meagre, still I hoped to be able to understand the original to the extent of telling where the translation failed to bring out the meaning. I began reading the *Gita* with them. The verses in the second chapter '... if one

Ponders on objects of the senses, there springs
Attraction; from attraction grows desire,
Desire flames to fierce passion, passion breeds
Recklessness; then the memory — all betrayed —
Lets noble purpose go, and saps the mind,
Till purpose, mind, and man are all undone.'

made a deep impression on my mind, and they still ring in my ears. The book struck me as one of priceless worth. The impression has ever since been growing on me with the result that I regard it today as the book *par excellence* for the knowledge of Truth. It has afforded me invaluable help in my moments of gloom.

THE *Gita* has been a mother to me ever since I became first acquainted with it in 1889. I turn to it for guidance in every difficulty, and the desired guidance has always been forthcoming. But you must approach Mother Gita in all reverence, if you would benefit by her ministrations. One who rests his head on her peace giving lap never experiences disappointment but enjoys bliss in perfection. This spiritual mother gives her devotee fresh knowledge, hope and power every moment of his life.

THE *Gita* says: 'Do your allotted work, but renounce its fruit. Be detached and work — have no desire for reward and work.' ... By detachment I mean that you must not worry whether the desired result follows from your action or not, so long as your motive is pure, your means correct. Really, it means that things will come right in the end if you take care of the means and leave the rest to Him.

THIS is the unmistakeable teaching of the *Gita*. He who gives up action falls. He who gives up only the reward rises. But renunciation of fruit in no way means indifference to the result. In regard to every action one must know the result that is expected to follow, the means thereto, and the capacity for it. He, who being thus equipped, without the desire for the result, and yet wholly engrossed in the due fulfilment of the task before him, is said to have renounced the fruit of his action.

THE last eighteen verses of the Second Chapter of the *Gita* give in a nutshell the secret of the art of living ... Those verses of the Second Chapter have since been inscribed on the tablet of my heart. They contain for me all knowledge. The truths they teach are the 'eternal verities'. There is reasoning in them, but they represent realized knowledge.

I have since read many translations and many commentaries, have argued and reasoned to my heart's content, but the impression that the first reading gave me has never been effaced. Those verses are the key to the interpretation of the *Gita*.

... TO me the *Gita* became an infallible guide of conduct. It became my dictionary of daily reference. Just as I turned to the English dictionary for the meaning of English words that I did not understand, I turned to this dictionary of conduct for a ready solution to all my troubles and trials. Words like *aparigraha* (non-possession) and *samabhava* (equability) gripped me. How to cultivate and preserve the equability was the question. How was one to treat alike insulting, insolent and corrupt officials, co-workers of yesterday raising meaningless opposition, and men who had always been good to one? How was one to divest oneself of all possessions? ... Was I to give up all I had and follow Him? Straight came the answer: I could not follow Him unless I gave up all I had.

MY study of English law came to my help ... I understood the *Gita* meaning of non-possession to mean that those who desired salvation should act like the trustee who, though having control over great possessions, regards not an iota of them as his own.

A TRUE votary of the *Gita* does not know what disappointment is. He ever dwells in perennial joy and peace that passeth understanding. But that peace and joy come not to the sceptic or to him who is proud of his intellect and learning. It is reserved only for the humble in spirit, who bring to her worship a fullness of faith and an undivided singleness of mind.

I HAVE not been able to see any difference between the Sermon on the Mount and the *Bhagavadgita*. What the Sermon describes in a graphic manner, the *Bhagavadgita* reduces to a scientific formula. It may not be a scientific book in the accepted sense of the term, but it has argued out the law of love — the law of abandon, as I would call it — in a scientific manner.

# On the South African Years, 1906-1914

SOUTH AFRICA is a representative of Western civilization while India is the centre of Oriental culture. Thinkers of the present generation hold that these two civilizations cannot go together. If nations representing these rival cultures meet even in small groups, the result will be an explosion. The West is opposed to simplicity while Orientals consider that virtue to be of primary importance. How can these opposite views be reconciled?

Western civilization may or may not be good, but Westerners wish to stick to it. They have shed rivers of blood for its sake. It is therefore too late for them now to chalk out a new path for themselves. Thus considered, the Indian question cannot be resolved into one of trade jealousy or race hatred. The problem is one of simply preserving one's own civilization.

The Indians are disliked in South Africa for their simplicity patience, perseverance, frugality, and other-worldliness. Westerners are enterprising, impatient, engrossed in multiplying their material wants and in satisfying them, fond of good cheer, anxious to save labour and prodigal in habits. They are therefore afraid that if thousands of Orientals settled in South Africa, the Westerners must go to the wall. Westerners in South Africa are not prepared to commit suicide and their leaders will not permit them to be reduced to such straits.

A MEMAN firm from Porbandar wrote to my brother making the following offer: 'We have business in South Africa. Ours is a big firm, and we have a big case there in the Court, our claim being £40,000. It has been going on for a long time.

We have engaged the services of the best *vakils* and barristers. If you send your brother there, he would be useful to us and also to himself. He would be able to instruct our counsel better than ourselves. And he would have the advantage of seeing a new part of the world, and of making new acquaintances.' *Gandhi was told*: 'It won't be a difficult job ... we have big Europeans as our friends, whose acquaintance you will make. You can be useful to us in our shop. Much of the correspondence is in English and you can help us with that too. You will, of course, be our guest and hence will have no expense whatever.'

'How long do you require my services?' I asked. 'And what will be the payment?'

'Not more than a year. We will pay you a first class return fare and a sum of £105, all found.'

This was hardly going there as a barrister. It was going as a servant of the firm. But I wanted somehow to leave India. There was also the tempting opportunity of seeing a new country, and of having new experience. Also I could send £105 to my brother and help in the expenses of the household. I closed with the offer without any hesitation and got ready to go to South Africa.

ON the seventh or eighth day after my arrival, I left Durban. A first class seat was booked for me ... The train reached Maritzburg, the capital of Natal, at about 9 p.m. Bedding used to be provided at this station. A railway servant came and asked me if I wanted any ... But a passenger came next and looked me up and down. He saw that I was a 'coloured' man.

This disturbed him. Out he went and came in again with one or two officials. They all kept quiet, when another official came to me and said, 'Come along, you must go to the van compartment.'

'But I have a first class ticket,' said I.

'That doesn't matter,' rejoined the other. 'I tell you, you must go to the van compartment.'

'I tell you, I was permitted to travel in this compartment at Durban, and I insist on going on in it.'

'No, you won't,' said the official. 'You must leave this compartment, or else I shall have to call a police constable to push you out.'

'Yes, you may. I refuse to get out voluntarily.'

The constable came. He took me by the hand and pushed me out. I refused to go to the other compartment and the train steamed away. I went and sat in the waiting room, keeping my hand bag with me, and leaving the other luggage where it was. The railway authorities had taken charge of it.

It was winter, and winter in the higher regions of South Africa is severely cold. Maritzburg being at a high altitudes, the cold was extremely bitter. My overcoat was in my luggage, but I dare not ask for it lest I be insulted again, so I sat and shivered. There was no light in the room ...

I began to think of my duty. Should I fight for my rights or go back to India, or should I go on to Pretoria without minding the insults, and return to India after finishing the case? It would be cowardice to run back to India without fulfilling my obligation. The hardship to which I was subjected was superficial, only a symptom of the deep disease of colour prejudice. I should try, if possible, to root out the disease and suffer hardships in the process. Redress for wrongs I would seek only to the extent that would be necessary for the removal of the colour prejudice.

So I decided to take the next available train to Pretoria.

THE train reached Charlestown in the morning. There was no railway, in those days, between Charlestown and Johannesburg, but only a stagecoach ... I possessed a ticket for the coach ... But the agent only needed a pretext for putting me off, and so, when he discovered me to be a stranger, he said: 'Your ticket is cancelled.' I gave him the proper reply. The reason at the back of his mind was not want of accommodation. Passengers had to be accommodated inside the coach, but I was regarded as a 'coolie' and looked a stranger, so it would be proper, thought the 'leader', as the white man in charge of the coach was called, not to seat me with the white passengers. There were seats on either side of the coachbox. The leader sat on one of these as a rule. Today he sat inside and gave me his seat. I knew it was sheer injustice and an insult, but I thought it better to pocket it ...

At about three o'clock the coach reached Pardekoph. Now the leader decided to sit where I was seated, as he wanted to smoke and possibly to have some fresh air. So he took a piece of dirty sack-cloth from the driver, spread it on the footboard and, addressing me, said: '*Sami*, you sit on this, I want to sit near the driver.' The insult was more than I could bear. In fear and trembling I said to him, 'It was you who seated me here, though I should have been accommodated inside. I put up with the insult. Now that you want to sit outside and smoke, you would have me sit at your feet. I will not do so, but I am prepared to sit inside.'

As I was struggling through these sentences, the man came down upon me and began heavily to box my ears. He seized me by the arm and tried to drag me down. I clung to the brass rails of the coachbox and was determined to keep my hold even at the risk of breaking my wristbones. The passengers were witnessing the scene — the man swearing at me, dragging and belabouring me, and I remaining still. He was strong and I was weak. Some of the passengers were moved to pity and exclaimed: 'Man, let him alone. Don't beat him. He is not to blame. He is right. If he can't stay there, let him come and sit with us.'

'No fear,' cried the man, but he seemed somewhat crestfallen and stopped beating me.

MY profession progressed satisfactorily, but that was far from satisfying me. The question of further simplifying my life and of doing some concrete act of service to my fellowmen had been constantly agitating me, when a leper came to my door. I had not the heart to dismiss him with a meal. So I offered him shelter, dressed his wounds, and began to look after him …

UP to the year 1906 I simply relied on appeal to reason. I was a very industrious reformer ... But I found that reason failed to produce an impression when the critical moment arrived in South Africa. My people were excited; even a worm will and does sometimes turn, and there was talk of wreaking vengeance. I had then to choose between allying myself to violence or finding out some other method of meeting the crisis and stopping the rot; and it came to me that we should refuse to obey the legislation that was degrading and let them put us in jail if they liked. Thus came into being the moral equivalent of war ... Since then the conviction has been growing upon me, that things of fundamental importance to the people are not secured by reason alone but have to be purchased with their suffering ... I have come to this fundamental conclusion, that if you want something really important to be done you must not merely satisfy the reason, you must move the heart also.

WHEN the Indian labourers of the north coast went on strike, the planters at Mount Edgecombe would have been put to great loss if all the cane that had been cut was not brought to the mill and crushed. Twelve hundred Indians therefore returned to work with a view to finish this part of the work, and joined their compatriots only when it was finished. Again, when the Indian employees of the Durban Municipality struck work, those who were engaged in the sanitary services of the borough or as attendants upon the patients in hospitals were sent back, and they willingly returned to their duties. If the sanitary services were dislocated, and if there was no one to attend upon the patients in hospitals, there might be an outbreak of disease in the city and the sick would be deprived of medical aid, and no *satyagrahi* would wish for such consequences to ensue. Employees of this description were therefore exempted from the strike. In every step that he takes, the *satyagrahi* is bound to consider the position of his adversary. I could see that numerous cases of such chivalry left their invisible but potent impress everywhere ...

ONE of General Smuts' secretaries said jocularly to me: 'I do not like your people, and I do not care to assist them at all. But what am I to do? You help us in our days of need. How can we lay hands upon you? I often wish that you took to violence like the English strikers, and then we would know at once how to dispose of you. But you will not injure even the enemy. You desire victory by self-imposed limits of courtesy and chivalry. And that is what reduces us to sheer helplessness.'

*Volksrust, 1913*
... WE passed a few happy days in Volksrust jail, where new prisoners came every day and brought us news of what was happening outside. Among these *satyagrahi* prisoners there was one old man named Harbatsinh who was 75 years of age. Harbatsinh was not working on the mines which the Indians had struck. He had completed his indenture years ago and he was not therefore a striker. The Indians grew far more

enthusiastic after my arrest, and many of them got arrested by crossing over from Natal into the Transvaal. Harbatsinh was one of these enthusiasts.

'Why are you in jail?' I asked Harbatsinh. 'I have not invited old men like yourself to court jail.'

'How could I help it,' replied Harbatsinh, 'when you, your wife, and even your boys went to jail for our sake?'

'But you will not be able to endure the hardships of jail life. I would advise you to leave jail. Shall I arrange for your release?'

'No, please. I will never leave jail. I must die one of these days, and how happy should I be to die in jail.'

It was not for me to try to shake such determination which would never have been shaken even if I had tried. My head bent in reverence before this illiterate sage. Harbatsinh had his wish and he died in Durban jail on January 5th, 1914.

### The Transvaal, 1914

I WENT to Pretoria with Andrews. Just at this time there was a great strike of the European employees of the Union railways, which made the position of the government extremely delicate. I was called upon to commence the Indian march at such a fortunate juncture. But I declared that the Indians could not assist the railway strikers, as they were not out to harass the government, their struggle being entirely different and differently conceived. Even if we undertook the march, we would begin it at some other time when the railway trouble had ended. This decision of ours created a deep impression, and was cabled to England by Reuter. Lord Ampthill (Secretary of the Colonies) cabled his congratulations. English friends in South Africa too appreciated our decision.

*South Africa, 1914*

WE thus reached a provisional agreeement after eight years of struggle and *satyagraha* was suspended for the last time ... It was rather difficult to get the Indians to endorse this agreement. No one would wish that enthusiasm which had arisen should be allowed to subside. Again, whoever would trust General Smuts? Someone reminded me of the fiasco in 1908 and said: 'General Smuts once played us false, often charged you with forcing fresh issues, and subjected the community to endless suffering. And yet what a pity that you have not learnt the necessary lesson of declining to trust him! The man will betray you once again, and you will again propose to revive *satyagraha*. But who will then listen to you?'

I knew that such arguments would be brought forth, and was not therefore surprised when they were. No matter how often a *satyagrahi* is betrayed, he will repose his trust in the adversary so long as there are not cogent grounds for distrust. Pain to the *satyagrahi* is the same as pleasure. He will not therefore be misled by the mere fear of suffering into groundless distrust. On the other hand, relying as he does upon his own strength, he will not mind being betrayed by the adversary, will continue to trust in spite of frequent betrayals, and will believe that he thereby strengthens the forces of truth and brings the victory nearer ... Distrust is a sign of weakness and *satyagraha* implies the banishment of all weakness and therefore distrust, which is clearly out of place when the adversary is not to be destroyed but to be won over.

IT is the acid test of nonviolence that in a nonviolent conflict there is no rancour left behind and, in the end, the enemies are converted into friends. That was my experience in South Africa with General Smuts. He started with being my bitterest opponent and critic. Today he is my warmest friend.

# On Food, Drink and Tobacco

THE process of eating is as unclean as evacuation, the only difference being that, while evacuation ends in a sense of relief, eating, if one's tongue is not held in control, brings discomfort. Just as we attend to evacuation in private, we should likewise eat and perform other actions common to all animals in private.

I DO not regard flesh food as necessary for us at any stage and under any clime in which it is possible for human beings ordinarily to live. I hold flesh food to be unsuited to our species. We err in copying the lower animal world if we are superior to it. Experience teaches that animal food is unsuited to those who would curb their passions.

VEGETARIANISM is one of the priceless gifts of Hinduism. It may not be lightly given up. It is necessary therefore to correct the error that vegetarianism makes us weak in mind or body, or passive or inert in action. The greatest Hindu reformers that have been most active in their generations have invariably been vegetarians.

I EAT to live, to serve and also, if it so happens, to enjoy, but I do not eat for the sake of enjoyment.

ONE should eat not in order to please the palate, but just to keep the body going. When each organ of sense subserves the body, and through the body the soul, its special relish disappears and then alone does it begin to function in the way that nature intended it to do so.

I HAVE known many meat eaters to be far more nonviolent than vegetarians.

A MAN who wants to control his animal passions easily does so if he controls his palate.

Fasting can help to curb animal passion, only if it is undertaken with a view to self-restraint. Some of my friends have actually found their animal passion stimulated as an after effect of fasts. That is to say, fasting is futile unless it is accompanied by incessant longing for self-restraint. The famous verse from the Second Chapter of the *Bhagavadgita* is worth noting in this connection:

'For a man who is fasting his senses
Outwardly, the sense objects disappear,
Leaving the yearning behind; but when
He has seen the Highest,
Even the yearning disappears.'

Fasting and similar discipline is, therefore, one of the means to the end of self-restraint, but it is not all, and if physical fasting is not accompanied by mental fasting, it is bound to end in hypocrisy and disaster.

FASTING is useful, when mind cooperates with starving body, that is to say, when it cultivates a distaste for the objects that are denied to the body.

OF what use is it to force the flesh merely if the spirit refuses to cooperate?  You may starve even unto death, but if at the same time the mind continues to hanker after objects of the sense, your fast is a sham and a delusion.

MORE caution and perhaps more restraint are necessary in breaking a fast than in keeping it.

DRINK is more a disease than a vice.  I know scores of men who would gladly leave off drink if they could.  Diseased persons have got to be helped against themselves.  The drink curse has desolated many a labourer's home.

ONLY those women who have drunkards as their husbands know what havoc the drink devil works in homes that were once orderly and peace loving.

NOTHING but ruin stares a nation in the face that is a prey to the drink habit.

YOUR capacity to keep your vow will depend on the purity of your life.  A gambler, or a drunkard, or a dissolute character can never keep a vow.

I HAVE a horror of smoking as I have of wines.  Smoking I consider to be a vice.  It deadens one's conscience and is often worse than drink in that it acts imperceptibly.  It is a habit to get rid when once it seizes hold of a person.  It is an expensive vice. It fouls the breath, discolours the teeth and sometimes even causes cancer. It is an unclean habit.

# On Women, Marriage, Sex and Birth Control

OF all the evils for which man has made himself responsible, none is so degrading, so shocking or so brutal as his abuse of the better half of humanity, to me, the female sex, not the weaker sex.

TO call a woman a member of the weaker sex is a libel. In what way woman is the weaker sex, I do not know. If the implication is that she lacks the brute instinct of man, or does not possess it in the same measure as man, the charge may be admitted. But then woman becomes, as she is, the nobler sex. If she is weak in striking, she is strong in suffering.

I HAVE regarded woman as the incarnation of tolerance. A servant wrongly suspected may throw up his job, a son in the same case may leave his father's roof, and a friend may put an end to the friendship. The wife, if she suspects her husband, will keep quiet, but if the husband suspects her, she is ruined.

MAN has converted her into a domestic drudge and an instrument of his pleasure, instead of regarding her as his helpmate and better half. The result is a semi-paralysis of society. Woman has rightly been called the mother of the race. We owe it to her and to ourselves to undo the great wrong we have done her.

I BELIEVE in the proper education of women. But I do not believe that woman will make her contribution to the world by mimicking or running a race with man. She can run the race but she will not rise to the great heights she is capable of by mimicking man. She has to be the complement of man.

WOMAN must cease to consider herself the object of man's lust.

MARRIAGE is a natural thing in life, and to consider it derogatory in any sense is wholly wrong. The ideal is to look upon marriage as a sacrament and therefore to lead a life of self-restraint in the married state.

I MUST declare with all the power that I can command that sensual attraction even between husband and wife is unnatural. Marriage is meant to cleanse the heart of the couple of sordid passions and take them nearer to God. Lustless love between husband and wife is possible. Man is not a brute.

WHEN a husband and wife gratify the passions, it is no less an animal indulgence on that account. Such an indulgence, except for perpetuating the race, is strictly prohibited.

THE wife is not the husband's bondslave, but his companion and his helpmate, and an equal partner in all his joys and sorrows — as free as the husband to choose her own path.

THE devotion of a servant was, I felt, a thousand times more praiseworthy than that of a wife to her husband. There was nothing surprising in the wife's devotion to her husband, as there was an indissoluble bond between them. The devotion was perfectly natural. But it required a special effort to cultivate equal devotion between master and servant.

IT is more necessary for a husband to draw closer to his wife when she is about to fall.

MY friend once took me to a brothel. He sent me in with the necessary instructions. It was all prearranged. The bill had already been paid. I went into the jaws of sin, but God in His infinite mercy protected me against myself. I was almost struck blind and dumb in this den of vice. I sat near the woman on the bed, but I was tongue-tied. She naturally lost patience with me, and showed me the door, with abuses and insults. I then felt as though my manhood had been injured, and wished to sink into the ground for the shame. But I have ever since given thanks to God for saving me. I can recall four more similar incidents in my life, and in most of them my good fortune, rather than any effort on my part, saved me. From a strictly ethical point of view, all these occasions must be regarded as moral lapses; for the carnal desire was there, and it was as good as the act. But from the ordinary point of view, a man who is saved from physically committing a sin is regarded as saved. And I was saved only in that sense.

THE conquest of lust is the highest endeavour of a man or a woman's existence.

MY meaning of *brahmachari* is this: One who by constant attendance upon God, has been capable of lying naked with naked women, however beautiful they may be, without being in any manner whatsoever sexually excited.

As an external aid to *brahmachari*, fasting is as necessary as selection and restriction in diet. So overpowering are the senses that they can be kept under control only when they are completely hedged in on all sides, from above and from beneath. It is common knowledge that they are powerless without food, and so fasting undertaken with a view to control the senses is, I have no doubt, very helpful.

THERE can be no two opinions about the necessity for birth control. But the only method handed down from ages past is self-control or *brahmacharya*. It is an infallible sovereign remedy doing good to those who practise it. And medical men will earn the gratitude of mankind, if, instead of devising artificial means of birth control, they will find out the means of self-control. The union is meant not for pleasure but for bringing forth progeny. And union is a crime when the desire for progeny is absent.

LOVE becomes lust the moment you make it a means for the satisfaction of animal needs.

ARTIFICIAL methods are like putting a premium upon vice. They make a man and woman reckless. And respectability that is being given to these methods must hasten the dissolution of the restraints that public opinion puts upon one. Adoption of artificial methods must result in imbecility and nervous prostration. The remedy will be found to be worse than the disease. It is wrong and immoral to seek to escape the consequences of one's acts. It is good for a person who over-eats to have an ache and fast. It is bad for him to indulge his appetite and then escape the consequence by taking tonics or other medicine. It is still worse for a person to indulge in his animal passions and escape the consequences of his acts. Nature is relentless and will have full revenge for any such violation of her law.

I THINK it is the height of ignorance to believe that the sexual act is an independent function like sleeping or eating. The world depends for its existence on the act of generation, and as the world is the playground of God and a reflection of His glory, the act of generation should be controlled for the ordered growth of the world. He who realises this will control his lust at any cost, equip himself with the knowledge necessary for, the physical, mental and spiritual well being of his progeny, and will give the benefit of that knowledge to posterity.